# 'Lord, I Believe . . .'

## The Power of God
## to Transform Your Life!

by
**Jim Ayers**
with
**Robert Mims**

www.xulonpress.com

# Dedication

I dedicate this book to my best friend and loving partner in life for nearly 38 years, Carrie. Without her encouragement and spiritual perspective I never would have seen this work come to completion.

# Acknowledgments

I want to say a special thank you to my dear friend Bob Mims *(http://mimsmedia.com)* who took rough copy and turned it into this readable format. I can only imagine the number of hours you dedicated to this project. Your use of words is inspiring to all who read your work. I thank God for you.

I also want to thank the wonderful people at Life Church in Salt Lake City, Utah *(http://lifechurchutah. com)* who have made this confession their own and have enthusiastically backed me in this project. I am grateful to God for the privilege of serving this committed fellowship.

# The Confession: A Prayer of Promise for All Believers

Nearly every Sunday morning, I ask the people of Life Church to join me in a special prayer. We simply call it "The Confession."

*Lord, I believe you've got something*
*special for me today.*
*I lay aside every distraction of my life.*
*I open my spirit to receive more of you.*
*I give you my need so I can receive your blessings.*
*Forgive me of every sin. Cleanse my*
*heart completely.*

*Make me pure so that I might receive your glory.*
*Lord, I believe you've got something*
*special for me today.*
*And I claim it in Jesus' name.*
*Amen!*

I first wrote those words in 1997, a time of personal distress and no small amount of anxiety. I had just gotten test results that showed elevated liver enzymes, and doctors had performed a biopsy. For six weeks, I waited to learn whether I had cancer. Eventually, things turned out well – but during that period of uncertainty, and in the years since for many other challenges life has brought, I found the words of *The Confession* both a comfort and a tool to building victorious faith.

My choice then was rather clear-cut: I could allow myself to sink deeper and deeper into a sea of worry and desperation – or I could claim the faith I preached every Sunday from my pulpit *for myself* as well as my congregation. In other words, I could fight back against the depression by claiming and really taking hold of what God has promised His children as their inheritance.

What has He offered us through our adoption into His family? Nothing less than forgiveness, eternal salvation, peace, joy, provision, blessing and His constant, loving companionship and guidance.

I knew my battered spirit needed those gifts at that time of doubt. So, in an attitude of prayer, I sat down and put those yearnings, petitions and expectations into words. I believe what resulted, though written by my hand, was inspired by a Heavenly Father who knew the needs of my heart more thoroughly and deeply than I could ever imagine.

I needed a straightforward declaration that would guide me into the right attitude, submitted to the Lord but also expectant. I needed to enlist my mind, body and soul into His purposes, yet not shrink from grasping the promises He had laid before me.

I needed to both hear a confession of my faith, as well as reaffirm it to God; I needed to be focused on the very life and power of Jesus Christ, my anchor in eternity as well as my true source of confidence for each day – each heartbeat – of my life on Earth.

It worked! Once the words appeared on paper, I put down my pen and spoke them aloud. With each repetition, I felt a growing expectation inside me about God's faithfulness – and ripples of peace and calm that became warm waves of assurance.

I also would discover that beyond just spiritually lifting for that moment or that day, this prayer – this declaration – released greater blessings from God into my life as the weeks, months and years followed. That was both, perhaps, unexpected, and something for which I remain gratefully amazed.

It began as solely a personal confession to guide me through tough times and to refocus my priorities on Christ. But not long after I wrote it and made it a regular part of my daily devotions, I knew I had to share this tool of faith.

So, one Sunday I incorporated it into a sermon I preached at the church my wife, Carrie, and I were pastoring at the time. The response was good, and I thought that would be that. I moved on to other sermons, other topics – and tucked my handwritten confession into the flyleaf of my Bible.

It was some years later, after Carrie and I became pastors at Valley Assembly of God (now Life Church), that the Lord resurrected that prayer. I had picked up my Bible and my eyes locked on those words I had written during my time of trial. I got a strong impression: *You need to share this with the people here, too.*

Well, OK, I thought. I can update that sermon; deliver it and move on, just as I had before. This time, though, the Lord definitely had something more in mind. The response from the congregation was so strong, showed such a hunger for *The Confession's* message that I decided to make it a centerpiece of our worship services from that point forward.

The impact of that decision has been far greater than I ever would have hoped. The people latched onto promises and principles so simply stated, and when we made *The Confession* available on printed cards and bookmarks the response was overwhelming. Literally thousands of copies have been printed and shared over the years, and *The Confession* has spread far behind the walls of our church.

Life Church members and visitors have spread the cards and bookmarks to friends and families across the nation, even into prisons and jails. Ministers and evangelists have discovered *The Confession* during visits to Life Church and gone on to share the message from pulpits literally around the country and the world.

*The Confession* is not just a tool for Sunday worship, however. I encourage people to say it aloud, in an attitude of prayer, every day of their lives. And, if they are facing a crisis or going through tough times, declaring their faith and commitment – and claiming God's promises – I recommend repeating it several times a day.

It just plain works. I've heard a stream of incredible testimonies to that fact: miracles of peace, provision, healing, economic and personal blessings, and much more.

*The Confession* is not some sort of magic spell to be recited, though. There is no *power* in the card, bookmark or simply repeating the words. However, *The Confession* does do this: it focuses our minds and faith on the One who does have the power to work miracles in our lives; it builds faith in us, and faith moves the hand of God.

All the glory goes to Jesus, whose teachings are the foundation of *The Confession*, and whose love and grace lead us by the hand into a deeper understanding, awareness and ability to receive the blessings of His Kingdom.

In the following pages, I will break *The Confession* down into its elements. I hope that in so doing, you will discover with greater clarity the truth and application of each phrase. It is my prayer that these simple words will build and release faith in all who read them and that God's favor will be the result.

*"Our faith is not in these words but in the truth they hold and the God behind the truth,"* as the Apostle Paul said in 2 Corinthians 1:10 (NIV). *"On him [Jesus] we have set our hope . . . ."*

And so I say it again, and I pray you will join me:

*"Lord, I believe you've got something special for me today. And I claim it in Jesus' name!"*

## Chapter One

# Lord, I Believe You've Got Something Special for Me

*"The unexamined life is not worth living."*

You have probably heard that expression, traditionally attributed to the Greek philosopher Socrates. But the concept is repeated throughout the Bible as well.

In the New Testament book of James, believers are warned about how easy it is to lose track of ourselves; he wrote that it was like a man who finds a mirror *"and after looking at himself, goes away and immediately forgets what he looks like."* (James 1:24 NIV).

So, let's examine our lives. What challenges are you facing? What miracles of faith do you need in your life, in your attitude toward the only One who can provide the answers?

Here are a few I've seen pop up with regularity in my years as a pastor:

- "The company has to make big cuts, they'll probably cut me."
- "I'm expecting the doctor's report to show something serious."
- "I don't expect my marriage to survive."
- "I doubt God could really forgive me."

I would be surprised if you or someone you love has not faced such challenges as these! I know from personal experience how prone *I* can be to expect the worst to happen instead of the best. But that can be a crippling way of thinking – and believing –

for a Christian *because fear thrives in that kind of environment.*

The Old Testament prophet Habakkuk had words from God about how to meet such negativity in life and thought:

"*. . . watch – and be utterly amazed. For I am going to do something in your days that you will not believe, even if you were told.*" (Habakkuk 1:5 NIV).

I really believe that God intends to astound and amaze us; that He wants to do among us something that takes us back and gets us to take notice – something so *extraordinary* that if He were to tell us about it we would struggle to believe it!

But that's what the life of faith will bring into your life.

If we're really going to start *winning* the challenges in our lives (rather than merely *enduring* them) we've got to move out of the "can't" frame of mind and into the "can" reality of the Spirit. We need to move into faith.

I want to tell you how important and exciting a life of faith – an attitude of belief and expectation – can be.

Faith is important because the Bible clearly states that, *". . . without faith it is impossible to please God, because anyone who comes to him must believe that he exists and that he rewards those who earnestly seek him."* (Hebrews 11:6 NIV).

Faith is exciting because Jesus himself declared, *". . . Everything is possible to him who believes."* (Mark 9:23 NIV).

Can't get much clearer than that now, can He? With faith, *all things are possible!* So, it follows that when *you* come to God with your concerns and ask for His answers in confidence and acceptance of His will for your life, *you must believe!*

Yes, faith is important, even vital, because the Word of God says you *must* have it. However, faith is exciting because Jesus said it is, when channeled through God's direction and your words of affirmation, *powerful.*

What did the Lord say about that power? *It can move mountains.* (Matthew 21:21). Go ahead, read that verse: *". . . if you have faith and do not doubt . . . you can say to this mountain, 'Go throw yourself into the sea,' and it will be done."*

Again, from God-centered faith comes *authority.*

And now another eye-opener: Faith is so important that the Lord tells us that whatever else we allow to wriggle into our decision-making process on matters of right and wrong behavior is a rejection of his lordship. *". . . everything that does not come from faith is sin."* (Romans 14:23 NIV).

But faith is exciting because Jesus clearly defined it as the irreplaceable key to unlocking the blessings He desires to give us. Consider what He told a group of desperate blind men who stumbled up to Him on the road, pleading for mercy and their sight (Matthew 9:27-30 NIV):

*"Do you believe that I am able to do this?"* he asked them. Yes! That was their answer; none of

today's attitude of *Well, theoretically, sure. If you want to, I suppose, you could.* No. The answer was an emphatic one of faith; the response of Jesus was just as emphatic!

*"Then he touched their eyes and said, 'According to your faith will it be done to you"; and their sight was restored. . . ."*

Some well-meaning, and yet misdirected, folks have tried to equate the amount of a person's faith with the "success" or "failure" of their prayers – as if there's some sort of magic formula that can squeeze compassion or blessing out of God. So, they argue, if God doesn't answer your prayers the way you want, then it's your own fault – obviously, you didn't have *enough* faith.

That attitude is wrong. It is not truly "of faith," and we know from earlier in this chapter what the Lord says about that.

No, it is *not* the amount or size of your faith that matters! It is the size of the *God you place your faith in* that is the whole point. If the Maker of the Universe

Himself is too small to you to rule and bless your life, hopes, dreams and future, then you will receive very little from Him.

Ah, but if He is a *big* God . . . get ready for miracles in your life and the lives of those you touch in your reaching out to them, and in prayer, for them.

Not long ago, Life Church hosted a meeting of 11 pastors of prominent evangelical Christian churches from the Greater Salt Lake Area. We shared our visions and dreams for our congregations – and for the work of Christ in the Salt Lake metropolitan area as a whole. Then, we prayed for each other, our churches and their people. Those men prayed for Life Church specifically, asking for God's divine provision and favor among us.

It was a powerful, humbling experience. All who attended could feel the anointing of the Holy Spirit on that gathering. That came because of our attitude toward each other, and our position before the Lord. We had laid those visions and dreams, written on paper, before the pulpit as if we were placing a sacrifice on the altar of God himself. It truly was holy ground for us that day.

One of the pastors that day told us about a miraculous act of provision his church has received. We were all in awe of what God had done for him and his congregation. I joked with him about being God's "favorite," and remarked, in jest, that the Lord had never done anything like that for me.

But instead of just laughing off my good-natured jibe, he answered with a comment that wiped the smile off my face and dug deeply into my soul. *"Well, have you ever asked God to do something like that for you?"*

Chagrined, I had to sheepishly admit that I had not. He then said, *"Well?"* Indeed. If I didn't *ask,* what DID I expect?

God is saying He wants to work in our lives in astounding ways. But we don't ask because so often we really don't have faith for it. Our problem? Our God is too small, at least in our own eyes. The only cure for that condition is to get a new vision of His power and glory and His desire to move among us through miracles.

He *wants* to astound us. And I believe He wants to *amaze* us individually, as families and as a church. Tell you what; I think God has His hand on Life Church, that He wants to use our congregation in a very significant way for His Kingdom in the Salt Lake Valley. And I think He wants to use *all* of his churches throughout the world!

Specifically, I feel He wants to usher in a new wave of His *fullness* operating in our lives, just as the prophet Joel said: *". . . I will pour out my Spirit on all people."* (Joel 2:28 NIV).

This is God's heart for His people, to flood them in a great outpouring of His love, Spirit and purpose – to show Himself to be truly *great* in our lives.

*"The eyes of the Lord search the whole earth, in order to strengthen those whose hearts are fully committed to him. . . ."* (2 Chronicles 16:9 NLT).

He is looking for *us*. He is looking for fully committed believers ready to be vessels for His blessings and tools for His work. For all of us who reach out with that kind of faith, there is something wonderful just over the horizon.

God *wants* to make us bearers of His miracle power – to show Himself to be great through *your* life!

We have been raised up for such a time as this, whatever that time or challenge is that we face individually, as families or a church. You, me, we are not here by accident. We are people of destiny. And we need to stir up the faith within and start believing God for bigger and greater things.

That is exactly what Jesus challenged us to do when he taught: *"I tell you the truth, anyone who believes in me will do the same works I have done, and even greater works, because I am going to be with the Father."* (John 14:12 NLT).

That kind of faith will affect each of us in three key ways:

### – **First, it will cause you to truly seek God.**

The kind of faith Jesus spoke about looks at circumstances that seem so out of control and turns resolutely toward God *because* nothing is out of *His* control. In other words, we simply must stop putting our God in a box!

It is human nature to try to define the unknown. If we can somehow *understand* the mysteries, then in some sense we can also control them – or so the thinking goes. But God, by His very nature, is far beyond our feeble reasoning. We can't put Him in a box; He *created* the ultimate "box" – the Universe – and even that cannot contain its Maker!

If we *could* put God in a box, He would *not* be God, would He? So, when we try to do that, we sabotage our faith – we limit the Lord (at least in the expectations of our minds and spirits) and our faith will wither. God-in-a-box faith presumes our Heavenly Father works the same way every time. He does not consult our little rule books for divine behavior, though; God is always changing – not His nature, but His methods and responses – to answer prayers as people's hearts, situations and needs change.

This unpredictable aspect of our Lord has been a frequent topic of discussion for Life Church's pastoral staff. We've come to the conclusion that one reason God changes His methods and ways from time to time may be this simple and yet profound: If we grew too accustomed to His ways of working in our lives, our passion for seeking Him may fade, even evaporate completely.

In other words, we would get spiritually lazy. Our growth as His children would stagnate, just like an athlete's muscles would atrophy if he or she stopped exercising completely.

More than anything, Jesus wants us to talk with Him, learn from Him and lean on Him. To encourage us to be consistent in that, He changes his "M.O." (method of operation) from time to time to make us seek Him, and not our own "understanding" of Him (which is, after all, almost always *wrong!*)

This has been the pattern of a patient and loving God going back thousands of years. One memorable example is that of a future king who took on a giant with nothing more than his sling, five stones and a whole lot of uncompromising faith. Of course, you have probably guessed I'm talking about David and Goliath, an encounter detailed in the Old Testament.

More than that, though, is an ongoing struggle between David's people, the Israelites, and Goliath's, the Philistines – a militaristic horde of sea-going invaders known for their brutality and demonic gods.

For centuries, the Philistines were a constant source of worry for ancient Israel, always giving God's people trouble. These clashes led to many battles, and Israel – often coinciding with the state of its faithfulness to God at the time – was either victorious over the Philistines, or oppressed by them. As king, David frequently found himself leading the warriors of Israel against some new Philistine invasion. The Bible recounts a couple of the more noteworthy of those battles in the book of 2 Samuel, chapter 5, verses 18-25 (NIV):

*"Now the Philistines had come and spread out in the valley of Rephaim; so David inquired of the Lord, 'Shall I go and attack the Philistines? Will you hand them over to me?'*

*"The Lord answered him, 'Go, for I will surely hand the Philistines over to you.'*

*"So David went to Baal Perazim, and there he defeated them. He said, 'As waters break out, the Lord has broken out against my enemies before me.' . . . The Philistines abandoned their idols there, and David and his men carried them off.*

*"Once more the Philistines came up and spread out in the valley of Rephaim; so David inquired of the Lord, and he answered, 'Do not go straight up, but circle around behind them and attack them in front of the balsam trees. As soon as you hear the sound of marching in the tops of the balsam trees,*

*move quickly, because that will mean the Lord has gone out in front of you to strike the Philistine army.' So David did as the Lord commanded him, and he struck down the Philistines all the way from Gibeon to Gezer."*

Here were two battles with the Philistines that resulted in two devastating defeats for them – but David's God-directed strategy in each was different. While His will and purposes are always served, God's tactics to achieve them are not. What was consistent, though – what led to David's victory in each case – is that he sought God's ways, not his own.

David did not assume that because God had acted in a certain way on one occasion that he would *always* move in the same fashion when the next challenge arose for his people. David only assumed – had faith – that God had answered, and the king sought God out to learn what *His* plan would be for the next battle.

The fact is, Jesus wants to do things for us quicker and greater than we either believe for or even imagine. We need to stop limiting His work in our lives with our pitifully small thinking and crippled ability to believe. If you and I believe God only for the small things – because we think and believe small – what can we expect to receive?

Perhaps you've reached the point where you tell yourself that God has never done a "great work" in your life, so why believe He will now, when a particularly big need or challenge looms in front of you? You likely will get what you expect, though; that kind of "faith" will hold you back and keep you from stepping toward God's offered hand of blessing.

You might be a "spiritual veteran," one who feels confident he or she has an idea about how God "works." You've decided that since you have this knowledge, it has become unnecessary to seek Him out; you already think you know how the answer will come to your prayers.

Well, *veteran,* time to go back to spiritual boot camp; you need a refresher course on how to believe outside the box – and especially the part about being vigilant in *following* rather than getting ahead of God and therefore out of His will.

True faith will cause you to seek God *more,* not less.

### – Second, faith will cause you to give God your best.

With all that God's getting ready to do in your life, it is time for you to give God your very best, to give Him your all.

Some years ago, I decided to run in a 10-kilo-meter race – 6.2 miles. Now, I had never run a race before in my entire life, but I thought this would be a good test to see just what kind of shape I was in as a middle-aged man. I also knew enough that if I expected to conquer this challenge, I would have to carefully pace myself; if I tried to bolt out of the starting line like a teen-aged sprinter, I'd soon be out of gas and never be able to cross the finish line.

Well, the starter's gun went off and so did I, along with a crowd of other runners. Some of those folks quickly surged into the lead, and I remember thinking: *Man, those people are in great shape and I'm just back here, plodding along.* But I kept it up, my own slower pace, and about three miles into the run – the halfway point – there were those same would-be star athletes, now walking or standing, out of breath as I ran by them.

All I had wanted to accomplish when I started that race was to run the entire distance, no matter how slowly; I wanted to cross the finish line knowing I had not walked or taken a break during any of the 6.2 miles. So, when I passed the 4 mile mark I was surprised to find myself under 40 minutes, a pace better than I had expected.

Suddenly, I knew I would not only meet my modest goal, but I actually had a chance to not only finish without walking – but to complete the race in under an hour's time. I got excited about the prospect, and as I passed the fifth mile, I noticed that without really thinking about it, I had actually picked up my pace! I still had something left in the tank, and I was accelerating toward the finish.

One way or another, we all know we are approaching our own finish line. We may be just starting the race, halfway through it, or have the final strides ahead of us. It could be our finish line will come with death and our graduation into His presence, or it may be that Christ will return and usher His children into His kingdom in what the Bible promises will be with a final heavenly trumpet blast and in the twinkling of an eye.

Either way, shouldn't your last mile be your best? Don't you want to cross your finish line in full stride, expending the last bit of energy in a burst of speed toward perfection?

Consider what the Apostle Paul wrote along this line in the New Testament book of Hebrews, where he discussed the quality of sacrificial giving as practiced by two sons of Adam and Eve – Cain and Abel. (You may recall the story from Genesis chapter 4, how Cain brought some of his crops as an offering, while Abel picked the first-born best of his flocks. Likely it was a matter of attitude as much as the form of sacrifice that resulted in God accepting Abel's sacrifice, but rejecting Cain's).

As Paul put it, *"By faith Abel offered unto God a more excellent sacrifice than Cain, by which he obtained witness that he was righteous...."* Hebrews 11:4 (KJV).

In other words, Abel did not settle for mediocrity in his service to God. He chose to serve Him with his whole heart, to give God the best of what he had. Abel didn't just serve the Lord on the Sabbath Day when others would see him; he didn't just serve God when he felt like it. Abel determined in his heart to give God his best. He committed to a life of excellence for the Lord.

We need more Abel attitudes today! Some of us have developed an attitude that we'll serve God so long as it isn't *inconvenient* ... or as long as life is good and we see a steady stream of blessings . . .

or as long as there is no price to be paid for our faithfulness.

Maybe that was what Cain's problem was, and he compounded that sin with one far worse when he killed his brother, Abel, rather than learning from his example. But whether thousands of years ago, or today, that kind of attitude isn't pleasing to the Lord. Our God is not interested in our leftovers, he wants our best.

He wants our *all*. When we offer that, he *will* bless us abundantly.

Now, if all you want to do is make it to heaven then I suppose you can invest just a minimal effort in serving God. You could just darken the door of Sunday services occasionally; tithe only when your finances are rolling along nicely; maybe you could even wink at those *little* sins cropping up in your life. After all, you are still *saved*.

But if what you yearn for is an intimacy with God, a faith that will move those mountains in your life and the lives of your loved ones, the minimal effort won't do. To be a person of faith – a person whose faith is not stagnant, but growing and reaching new levels of excellence in your service to the Lord – will require a higher effort; you will need to give God your best.

I know that *my goal* is not to just make it to heaven. I want to live my life full of the kind of faith that vibrates with the power of the Holy Spirit. I want to see God doing extraordinary things through my life; I want to see my prayers move the hand of God.

Most of all, I want to get to heaven not empty-handed, but with trophies to lie at the feet of Jesus and hear Him say, *"Well done, thou good and faithful servant."*

**– Third, faith causes us to expect miracles.**

You can never out-give God. It's a simple equation: You give Him your faith; He will give you your miracle.

Consider the example of a Roman centurion's simple, straight-forward and uncompromising faith as told in Matthew 8:5-13 (NIV). This man, a gentile, proved to be a marvel to Jesus.

The centurion's servant was very ill and near death, so this commander of soldiers himself went to find the Lord as He traveled through Capernaum. There, he approached Jesus, explained the situation and asked for His help.

*"Jesus said to him, 'I will go and heal him."* The Lord was ready to help, but then came an example of faith that was very rare: the centurion, this man who literally had the power of life and death over the Roman Empire's Jewish subjects, told Jesus that he was not worthy to have Jesus in his home.

*"But just say the word, and my servant will be healed,"* the centurion said. *"For I myself am a man under authority with soldiers under me. I tell this one 'Go,' and he goes, and that one, 'Come,' and he comes. I say to my servant, 'Do this,' and he does it.'"*

Jesus, the scripture tells us, was astonished. *"[He] said to those following him, "I tell you the truth, I have not found anyone in Israel with such great faith."*

Earlier in this chapter, I quoted the prophet Habakkuk and his promise that God would astound and amaze us with His blessings and provision for children of faith. Now, let me ask you: Have you, like the centurion in the story above, ever *astounded* Jesus with *your* faith?

Have you asked for a relationship with Him, a dependence upon Him that is larger, bigger and exponentially growing?

How about it? Let's astonish Jesus with our faith! If you need a miracle, God is ready to respond to *your* faith.

## Chapter Two

# I Lay Aside Every Distraction of My Life

Have you ever gone to your knees, intent on praying through on a particular issue – only to suddenly, almost without remembering when and how it occurred, find your thoughts have shifted to something else? It's like driving down a road, taking your eye off the road for one second, and next thing you know you've passed your exit and entered another state.

*Distraction.* Truth is, it is one of the most effective weapons the Enemy can deploy against us, and he does his best to do just that whenever he and his minions notice us praying. It's completely to Satan's benefit, and certainly none of our own, to have our minds racing *anywhere* but where they should be when we pray: at the throne of God.

Such distractions can be the toxic fruit of lives filled with just too much – too many projects, too many bills, too many possessions and the consequence of all that, too many worries.

The Apostle Paul knew a lot about this. In a letter to the believers in Corinth he encouraged them to avoid living such complicated lives. Paul wrote:

*"I want you to do whatever will help you serve the Lord best, with as few distractions as possible."* (1 Corinthians 7:35 NLT)

Let's be honest with each other. We *know* most of us have lives that are way too complicated. It's the American Dream become the American Nightmare. We have developed a culture where if we are not going a hundred different directions all at once and all the time, we're failing.

Of course, that is just not true. The truth is that we have so complicated our lives that we have become distracted into ineffectiveness. This truth applies as well to the life of the Spirit as well as your career, family or other temporal or day-to-day concerns.

One of the most important things you can do for your spiritual growth is to learn to develop a focused life. The Apostle Paul made it clear that we serve the Lord best when we do it with as few distractions as possible; in other words, when we serve him with a *focused* life.

Consider these words of wisdom from King Solomon: *"Look straight ahead, and fix your eyes on what lies before you."* (Proverbs 4:25 NLT)

That's pretty clear, isn't it? It is *very* important what you focus on in your life. The truth: When you know the right direction for your life, it is critical that you keep your spiritual eyes locked on that goal.

Now we all have known *distracted* people. Think about that: are they *ever* satisfied? They are always looking for the perfect job, the perfect marriage – the perfect church. They are always looking such things but never finding them.

Well, of course they aren't. They are distracted. They aren't looking *straight ahead;* they don't have their eyes fixed on what lies before them. If you try to steer a car through traffic, or sail a boat through a storm with such lack of vision and focus, you can guarantee yourself that you not only won't reach the destination – you'll crash or crash into the rocks and sink!

If we are to achieve in life, and if we are in that life to achieve great things for the Lord, we have got to learn to *discipline* our minds to fight the distractions and fix our eyes on what God has for us. Indeed, we must master and *overcome* distractions.

There is no greater example of this principle than the nation of Israel. Talk about distracted living – even after seeing God's faithfulness and provision for 40 years in the desert that followed Israel's deliverance and exodus from Egyptian slavery and oppression.

God forged a nation from those slaves, providing all their needs, fighting their battles, healing their diseases for an entire generation. Yet, despite the miracles they saw regularly, they repeatedly fell prey to distractions. *Where is our water, we'll perish of thirst!* God provided springs from rock. *Where's our food? We'd been better off as slaves back in Egypt, where at least we'd have something to eat!* God rained manna from the skies. *We're tired of this manna! We want some meat!* God filled the horizon of their Sinai campsites with quail. Ah. Manna for bread and game hens for meat. Yum.

Then — despite having witnessed God's hand in defeating the world's military power, drowning Pharaoh's charioteers in the Red Sea, and later intervening to give the fledgling nation victory over the war-like Amalakites – the Israelites got distracted with fear about their prospects of overthrowing the kingdoms opposing them in the Promised Land.

God had given His word to them – proven repeatedly by those past battles and challenges of survival in the wilderness – that He would take care of them. Repeatedly, He promised He would provide their needs, fight their battles, and give them the inheritance He had promised to their fathers Abraham, Isaac and Jacob.

Just obey and keep focused, I will do the rest. Trust in your God, was the simple requirement. Instead, they allowed their worries to overcome them and weaken their focus and resolve. Their faith eventually was so diminished that they became worthless to God, who then had to wait for a new generation – one hardened by 40 years of complete dependence on Him, focused in their faith on victory, not fear – to finally bring Israel into Canaan.

The enemy of our souls doesn't care what promises you think you have received from God. *Distraction,* his greatest weapon against the people of the Lord, has worked before to keep those promises from being received. Satan, unfortunately, is still using that weapon successfully against God's people millennia later.

Here four primary distractions the enemy uses today to get our focus off God and neutralize our faith:

– *Trials.* When you are going through a trial it is hard to see ahead to victory. That is because trials often dominate our lives emotionally and even physically; we are robbed of peace and hope and even the rest our bodies need. The trials can capture all our attention.

One of the first trials the Israelites faced after leaving Egypt had to do with water. Instead of trusting God, they complained. He provided water miraculously, but was disappointed in their lack of faith. He kept on providing for them, even when they rebelled and faced punishment; a patient God wanted the experience of provision, given time and again, to finally build faith that could not be shaken.

He wanted them to learn this lesson: God always responds to our faith, and the only thing that will limit what God can do in our lives *is* our faith. So, fight the good fight of faith; to do that, we have got to keep our eyes *off* our trials and *on* God's promises!

– *Delays*. The enemy will use delays to erode our faith. He won't necessarily be the *cause* of the delays, but Satan is the ultimate opportunist and will use them – anything, really – to get us to question God's faithfulness.

The nature of our society today makes distraction an even more effective strategy for the enemy. Think about it: ours is an *instant* society. We have instant potatoes, instant popcorn, and instant oatmeal (and even waiting for those items to cook for a minute or two in the microwave isn't fast enough for some!) We get irritated if it takes more than 60 seconds to order, receive and drive off with a hamburger from the local fast food restaurant's drive-up window.

So we Christians tend to expect the spiritual equivalent. We drive up to the window of heaven, shout our prayer into a cosmic speaker and then drive away in a huff if the answer isn't *instant* – and to our liking. With our food, our loved ones, our careers and our spiritual needs, we are always in a hurry!

Well, news flash: God is *not* in a hurry. He has His perfect time for everything – and every prayer request – because He wants to bring the *right* answer at just the *right* time. Oh, He knows how our minds work and how weak our faith can be, but *nothing* you do will force Him to take action any swifter than He wills.

*"God has given them a desire to know the future. He does everything just right and on time, but people can never completely understand what he is doing."* (Ecclesiastes 3:11 NCV).

So in other words, we have got to trust God's good and perfect timing and learn to be patient. Again, God does everything right and on time.

*Patience* is not a human strength, and lack of patience probably will plague us all the days of our earthly existence. Nonetheless, it is *patience* God requires of us; it goes hand-in-hand with effective faith, because it is the essence of trust.

– *Temptation*. The enemy also will use tempta-tion as a powerful distraction. In my years of ministry I've known Christians – lay people and ministers of the gospel alike – who receive astounding blessings from God, truly miraculous answers to prayer, only to throw it all away by giving in to one temptation or another.

Jesus spoke about this deadly distraction of temp-tation in the Gospel of Mark, comparing those who yield to it to seed scattered on thorny soil:

*". . . all too quickly the attractions of this world and the delights of wealth, and the search for suc-cess and lure of nice things come in and crowd out God's message from their hearts, so that no crop is produced."* (Mark 4:19 Living Bible)

Yielding to temptations crowd out God's favor in our lives. Temptations can snuff our trust in Him. Temptations can sweep us away from intimacy with the Lord, making Him truly distant to us – and leaving us just a crumbling shell of what may have once been a vibrant, promising and victorious Christian life.

What does it take to be a true disciple of Jesus? Part of faith, trust and keeping focus on goal is avoiding distractions, and the lure of temptations can be a detour from the course God has set us to follow in His service. Temptations always offer a seeming reward for a moral or ethical lapse: sexual pleasure, wealth, fame, power, selfish ambitions of all kinds.

But the Lord wants us to know those "rewards" are pleasures that are short-lived, not eternal in value, and ultimately worthless.

*"And how do you benefit if you gain the whole world but lose your own soul in the process? Is anything worth more than your soul? For I, the Son of Man, will come in the glory of my Father with his angels and will judge all people according to their deeds."* (Matthew 16: 26-27 NLT).

Sure, temptations can be strong foes, hard to resist. Satan knows exactly our weakest points and will make sure we are challenged in just those areas. But listen, temptations *can be overcome*. This is what God's Word says:

*"But remember that the temptations that come into your life are no different from what others experience. And God is faithful. He will keep the temptation from becoming so strong that you can't stand up against it. When you are tempted, he will show you a way out so that you will not give in to it."* (1 Corinthians 10:13 NLT).

– *Routine.* The enemy will use the routine of our lives to keep us preoccupied and off-focus. That's why you've got to have a daily prayer and devotional time. It is in those dedicated, focused times of seeking God that He takes you past the *routine* and gives you a dream for your life. If you never spend time with Him – in His Word or in prayer – you'll never receive that dream and you'll live your life mastered by distractions, instead.

The gospels tell us about two women who were disciples of Jesus, and yet they were – though sisters – as different in temperament as night and day. Mary was totally focused on Jesus and His words, dropping everything to be at His feet when He visited their home. Martha was just as devoted to the Lord, but she was more task-oriented by nature, and thus easily distracted.

Martha was so into her preparations and being the perfect hostess that one day she just plain got ticked off with her sister. You can see her, frantic with her *routine,* and her irritation with Mary boiling over as she took her complaint to Jesus himself.

*"[Mary] sat down at the feet of the Lord and listened to his teaching. Martha was upset over all the work she had to do, so she came and said, 'Lord, don't you care that my sister has left me to do all the work by myself? Tell her to come and help me!'*

*"The Lord answered her, 'Martha, Martha! You are worried and troubled over so many things, but just one is needed. Mary has chosen the right thing, and it will not be taken away from her.'"* (Luke 10:38-42 NLT)

Certainly, the routine of life has to be taken care of. Jesus was not saying it did not; He was, however, putting priorities and perspective in place for Martha (and us!). *Routine* must never be allowed to take the place of what's truly best for our lives: God's dream for us.

And of course, that is exactly why the Enemy will try to use life's *routines* to distract us and knock us off spiritual balance.

All of the distractions we've discussed are really a *test of our character.* How we respond will reveal where we really are inside. God allows these tests to come because they serve to develop us and change us.

If we pass these tests of character, God prepares us for blessings and service to Him at a higher level. If we do not pass, however, we will stay right where we are until we do; the tests will continue, probably bringing slightly different challenges – but still addressing the same trouble spots in our spiritual lives.

If your character flaw involves *patience,* then be sure you will face testing again, and again, and again in that area. It's like when, frustrated with the rush-hour commute on the freeway, we dart in and out of lanes seeking some escape. Seldom does that work – we simply find a new place to slow down and creep along, while the cars in the old lane suddenly are passing you by.

Perhaps this example rings a sharper clang in your experience: You will be in a hurry to check out at the store and, of course, you discover your clerk is the trainee. He or she is taking twice – no *three* – times as long as the veterans in the other lines to ring up customers and get them out the door.

Or, maybe this one resonates more: You are heading toward an appointment, already late, and you seem destined – or *cursed* – to *every* red light at *every* intersection.

You get the point. Life is filled with tests of our spiritual resolve, our *patience*. If you pass these tests, God takes you to a new level; He will bless you in new ways, and He will be able to use you more effectively for building His Kingdom. *But if you don't pass, you WILL be repeating this grade.*

When God gives us a dream, following it can bring both amazing miracles into our lives – and a painful price to pay. Consider Joseph, a young man who had a wonderful dream from the Lord, but one that stirred a near-murderous jealousy in his brothers. They were so offended and envious of God's blessings on their younger brother that they ambushed him, tossed him in a pit and then sold him into slavery.

Joseph certainly was in anguish over this betrayal by his own blood. As he was led away by Ishmaelite traders and sold again to an Egyptian, he must have played the scene over and over in his mind. But in the end, he resolved *not* to be overwhelmed by bitterness and anger – he chose to cultivate a right attitude, to trust God and believe in the dream God had given him.

God honored that, turning Joseph's situation completely around. Joseph may have begun his sojourn in Egypt as just another slave with a rope around his neck, but before God was done with him, he was holding the reins of Pharaoh's chariot, wearing his royal ring of authority, and second only to the Pharaoh in ruling over what was then the world's most powerful empire.

Later, when his brothers trembled in fear before him, fearful the brother they so wronged would take revenge upon them, Joseph instead had this to say to them:

*"As far as I am concerned, God turned into good what you meant for evil. He brought me to the high position I have today so I could save the lives of many people."* (Genesis 50:20 NLT).

Joseph forgave them. Instead of vengeance, he offered embraces and tears of joyful reunion. He provided for those brothers and their families during a time of famine. Joseph was at peace with trusting God, and believing in the dream.

The same can and should be true for us. Whatever the Enemy means for evil in our lives God will use for our good – for our promotion – if we'll live for Him and overcome the distractions.

There's only one way to overcome distractions. We have to give Jesus Christ first place in our lives. I know, many of us have heard that for years, but it is time for us to seriously consider what that means. How can we open our hearts to putting God's purpose in front of our spiritual eyes? How should we truly make His dream for us *our* dream? When will we put His purposes in the lead?

What do I mean by *first place?* It's all about *impact*. Let me put it this way: Everyone knows when you erect a building you start first with the foundation. For most of us, that is not the most impressive part of a construction project; after all, when the building is done, the foundation is hidden. No, we like to look at the walls, the roof lines, ceilings, paint, and carpet – the visible features that define architectural beauty.

But if you build those walls and the rest *before* laying down a solid, strong foundation, forget about the *beauty*. No building looks beautiful when it comes crashing down!

Sadly, that is an apt metaphor for so many people's lives. They have focused on building lives that seem so desirable, filled with possessions and wealth that shout "success." Then, inevitably, one of life's hurricanes or floods come along. Without a strong spiritual foundation, the beautiful lives they have so carefully nurtured – eroded by drugs, illicit sex, alcohol, maybe even depression and suicide – collapses into rubble.

They did not put the first things first. They didn't lay the foundation of life with the reinforced concrete and steel of God's purposes; instead of accepting Jesus as first in their lives and catching on to His dream, they chose a nightmare of their own making.

The collapse doesn't happen right away. For years, the *life house* built without Jesus as its foundation can look real good. Indeed, the fact that is does seem so desirable can be the biggest distraction of all. It can become an obsession, putting so much time into acquiring this decoration or adding that new room or landscaping.

It becomes easy to forget that underneath it all, there is no foundation, something we may not realize until it is too late.

Does this strike a chord with you? Let me ask you: Is Jesus really first in *your* life? Is He your foundation?

Or are you really just building your life for show?

## Chapter Three

# I Open My Spirit to Receive More of You

"*The spirit of the Lord will come upon you with power, and you . . . will be changed into a different person.*" (1 Samuel 10:6 NLT).

Do you hunger for more of God in your life? You should. I know that many people who have made Life Church their spiritual home came here because they found themselves empty and wanting more of the Lord; they came seeking an infilling of Christ's love and God's purpose and just knew there had to be more to life than the daily grind of working for material gain and weekends spent in chasing after the world's entertainments and escapes.

So the very people you may find sitting next to you in a Life Church worship service – maybe even you – took the chance one Sunday and came in our doors. And God touched you; it was like truly coming home.

The church didn't touch you, and it didn't change how you felt inside. That was God himself. *He* touched you. *He* forgave your sins. *He* set you free from the terrible things that bound you body, mind and spirit. *He* restored your marriage.

*He* gave you hope and a future.

Great as all that has been, though, deep inside you have wondered: Is this all there is, or does God have more for my life?

Oh, yes! He does have more, much more. I want to tell you with all the conviction I can muster that God's *more* will be just as exciting and powerful and fulfilling as anything you've received so far. He has more in store for you – *if* you will reach out for what He is offering.

Some Christians never experience God's big dream for their lives because they allow themselves to sink into a comfortable (and dull) existence as a *religious Christian.* That can easily happen to any one of us; anyone, even ministers, can tumble into this spiritual rut: we may know Christ as our Savior but the relationship with Him has grown stale since that initial joyous rush of invitation and forgiveness.

I've heard the same thing from couples I've counseled about their marriages. *"We just grew apart,"* one spouse will say. *"We fell out of love,"* another will claim. Or, yes, even those exact words as above: *"Our relationship has become stale."*

In my experience, though, what almost always has really happened in these cases is that such couples at the crossroads have just taken their marriages for granted – they have just quit working at it anymore. That attitude will never work in a marriage; any couple will "fall out of love" if they don't work at keeping their marriage healthy, fresh and moving forward.

It is no different in our relationship with God. You simply cannot afford to take it for granted, ignoring Him through the week and then thinking a couple hours on Sunday will set everything right. It won't happen; the relationship will grow stale.

Oh, you may still warm a seat on Sundays, even pay your tithes, but you will someday realize your relationship with God has become a distant, religious counterfeit for a living, vibrant relationship with Him. It will have lost that *sparkle* – the kind of crisis that the Apostle Paul warned about in 2 Timothy 3:5, where you have only a *"form of godliness"* that is spiritually empty; God's power isn't really touching your life anymore.

It does not have to be that way. It will be that way, though, unless you find a way to believe God for more in your life – and just as importantly, *open your spirit* to receive His dream, His discipline, His guidance and His blessings.

When I was a young boy in Indiana, we had a cistern in our back yard. A cistern is a rain trap, used to store water in areas where access to public water systems and pipelines may be a luxury. In our case, it was really little more than a deep hole we had once, years before, used to collect water for use in the home.

For me and my friends, though, it was a great place to put the tadpoles we captured from a nearby creek. In the cistern, they would grow into frogs, and we were fascinated by the process. Of course, among country boys tadpoles in the cistern was not that unusual of an event.

I recall an old story about a little frog that was born at the bottom of a small cistern. He and his frog family lived there together, and this slimy little green critter was content. He would play at ease, his family close by at all times, and felt pretty safe there in that sheltered cistern, which he knew like the back of his flippers.

*Life just doesn't get any better than this,* he thought. *I've got it made in this cistern; I have all I need!*

Then one day, the little frog looked up from the bottom and saw the sunlight pouring in from the distant top of his cistern world. His curiosity began to grow. *What is up there?* He wondered. Finally, our amphibian friend could no longer resist: he began to climb up the side of the cistern.

He got to the top and peered over it, astounded to see a pond nearby. Why, that pond made his cistern look rather paltry by comparison; there before his bulging eyes beckoned a body of water and lily pads a thousand times bigger than his home! *That's for me,* he told himself, and hopped out of the cistern and splashed into the pond with an explorer's delight.

But after a while, he looked around and saw that beyond his pond was a huge lake. This lake made the pond look like a mud hole, so off he hopped again, amazed – until, peering into the distance, the little frog saw the ocean, stretching endlessly into the hazy horizon.

He hopped and hopped and hopped some more, but finally the little frog found himself riding the ocean's waves. Everywhere he looked was water! Why, floating in this seemingly limitless sea, he realized just how limited he had been when he thought life and his dreams were contained within that cistern. Quite literally, what he had been ready to settle for was really just a drop in the bucket compared to what was possible for him to enjoy.

That is what our relationship with God is like. We are mere mortals, as the expression goes, creations living in Time for a specified number of heart beats between birth, life and inevitable death. Our God is infinite, eternal, the creator of Time and the universe, the Being who sees Past, Present and Future and every potential decision and crossroads along them, as a single, unified vision – His vision, His dream for us.

He simply is beyond our comprehension – without beginning or end, without limitations, beyond Time and Space. So, if you really think you have experienced all God has for you, you are sadly mistaken.

It does not matter who you are or how long you have walked in service to God. It doesn't matter how *deep* you think you are in your experience with Him – there is *still* more for you. Believe for more; seek His Spirit and His provision in your life.

In the book of 1st Samuel, the Bible recounts how the insecurities and doubts of a king ultimately led to his downfall. Saul, the first king of Israel, was chosen to lead a nation by God himself! But Saul's reaction to the news when it came from the prophet Samuel was not what you might expect.

Saul was not thrilled, at all. By nature timid and unsure of himself and the God of Israel, he protested his selection, even as Samuel poured anointing oil over his head.

*". . . am I not a Benjaminite, from the smallest tribe of Israel, and is not my clan the least of all the*

clans of the tribe of Benjamin? Why do you say such a thing to me?" (1 Samuel 9:21 NIV).

In other words, Saul' response to God's favor was basically, *What? Me? Who am I that God would choose me? Samuel, you must be mistaken, big time! I just don't have the chops for this job! King? No, no, no – I can't do this!*

OK, it's pretty easy to "tsk tsk" at Saul, isn't it? But haven't we all had such moments – indeed, maybe a lot of moments like those – where God spoke to our hearts about doing something for Him, and we shook our heads, stammering about how whatever it was, it was *too much for us*.

I can tell you that there have been many times in my life that God opened doors I just didn't want to walk through. Like Saul, I felt I couldn't do that particular task or take on that specific challenge. *I was not qualified.* At least, that is what I had convinced myself was the truth.

Of course, that fearful, doubting reaction is not where Saul's story ended. However, reluctantly, he finally agreed to God's plan and turned from a man looking for lost livestock into the king of the Lord's chosen nation. And once Saul surrendered to his destiny, something amazing happened.

*"When Saul and his servant arrived at Gilbeah, they saw a group of prophets coming toward them. Then the Spirit of God came powerfully upon Saul, and he, too, began to prophesy."* (1 Samuel 10:10 NLT).

God equipped Saul to do something he never imagined he could or would do. He can do the same for you.

Let's pray, though, that once you do allow God to take you by the hand, you don't later swell with pride and let go. That is, sadly, what Saul did. He made a series of bad choices with his life and God's Spirit of blessing left him.

The Bible tells us that instead of that spirit of blessing, a different, much darker spirit became Saul's companion – and tormentor. It filled the king with fear, left him deeply depressed and even prone to murderous fits of jealousy and rage.

God's Spirit of blessing found a new place to dwell, in the heart and life of a young shepherd boy, David. The day came when Samuel, having told the fallen King Saul that God's favor had been withdrawn from him, was once again marking royalty.

*". . . Samuel took the flask of olive oil he had brought and anointed David with the oil. And the Spirit of the Lord came powerfully upon David from that day on."* (1 Samuel 16:13 NLT).

Later in the same book, the Bible recounts that David *"was successful in all he did."* As long as David was faithful – as long as God's dream was also David's dream – the Lord was with him.

The impact of God's favor was in immediate evidence, too. When he was tending his father Jesse's sheep, on separate occasions a bear and a lion attacked the flock. David was not only able to chase them off, he killed the powerful beasts. Later, even though he was just a teenager, God's Spirit – and a sling with five small stones – was all he needed to down a giant, armored Philistine, Goliath.

He went out to face this warrior, who had the soldiers in King Saul's army literally shaking in their sandals, with full confidence in God. He approached the 9-foot-tall, professional killer infuriated over Goliath's mocking of Israel and its God, and full of passion for the honor of both.

Picture the shepherd boy, slowly twirling his sling as he approached the giant, telling the sneering man-mountain that he was about to die.

*". . . You come to me with sword, spear, and javelin, but I come to you in the name of the Lord Almighty—the God of the armies of Israel, whom you have defied.*

*"Today the Lord will conquer you, and I will kill you and cut off your head. And then I will give the dead bodies of your men to the birds and wild animals, and the whole world will know that there is a God in Israel! And everyone will know that the Lord does not need weapons to rescue his people.*

*"It is his battle, not ours. The Lord will give you to us!"* (1 Samuel 17:45-47 NLT).

That is exactly what happened in the next few minutes, as David unleashed a stone. Guided by the hand of God, it flew right to one of the few inches of the giant not protected – a tiny spot right between the eyes. Down Goliath came, out cold, as David then picked up the giant's own sword and lopped off his head.

The Philistines, seeing their champion dead and headless in the dust, ran. The Israelites chased them, cutting them down by the thousands. It was a great and unexpected victory – except in the heart of one shepherd boy.

Israel had found a hero, and as David grew and became a commander in the continuing battles with his nation's enemies, God blessed him time and again. David became so successful on the battlefield that when he returned each time in triumph, his fame grew – and Saul's diminished.

*"Saul has killed his thousands but David has killed his tens of thousands!"* they would cry.

God wants to do the same thing for you. He wants you to trust in Him, faithfully facing the giants in your life – confident, like David, that He will cause you to succeed in conquering those seemingly impossible mountains in your path.

Yes, God wants you to *excel* in your life by letting His Spirit fill you to overflowing. Your part? You have got to believe that God has *more in store for you.* Then, you must open your spirit – your life, dreams, hopes and desire to do things His way – to receive more of God.

This is what the Lord has promised us:

*In the last days,* [that's Bible language for the time just before the return of Jesus Christ, the time when He comes back to get us] *God says, 'I will pour out My Spirit upon all people. Your sons and daughters will prophesy. Your young men will see visions, and your old men will dream dreams. In those days I will pour out My Spirit even on My servants — men and women alike. . . ."* (Acts 2:17-18 NLT).

This promise from the Lord – and whether you embrace and act on it – is the difference between defeat and victory, weakness and power, ineffectiveness and effectiveness, fear and faith, cowardice and courage. This promise is reserved for every spiritually hungry heart, every open heart, and every longing heart.

That is what is at the heart of *The Confession.* When we say it, when we *pray* it, we are opening out hearts and spirits to *receive more of God.* We do this even as we acknowledge that we *need* more of the Holy Spirit in our lives.

It is as simple – and powerful – as that. We admit we need more, and we acknowledge that we want more!

Back to Moses for a bit. Now, you'd think that once the Israelites saw God part the Red Sea *and* drown an army of Pharaoh's finest, things would calm down some. Maybe, the rest of the trip to the

Promised Land would be less . . . eventful. Forget about it. Instead, this nation-on-the-move encountered one big issue after another. They quickly learned that they simply were not going to make it without God's help.

One day, Moses had a conversation with God about it all. The Bible recounts part of that exchange:

*"The Lord replied, 'My Presence will go with you, and I will give you rest.' Then Moses said to him, 'If your Presence does not go with us, do not send us up from here.'"* (Exodus 33:14-15 NIV).

It was pretty clear what Moses' conclusion was: If God doesn't make this trip with us, we are *doomed*. Isn't it the same with us? Personally, I can think of some very significant times in my life, some critical crossroads of decision where I went to my knees and cried out: *"Father, if you don't go with me, don't send me any farther. I've got to have your Presence with me! I need more of you."*

That's all the Lord is looking for from us. He cherishes people who will honestly admit they need more of Him, that they long for more of His Spirit in their lives.

That is what it means when we *confess* the words: *"I open my spirit to receive more of you."* In saying that, in *meaning* that, we are acknowledging that God's got more in store for our lives – and that we are hungry to receive it.

Are you ready to feast on the blessings of the Lord's Presence?

## Chapter Four

# I Give You My Needs So I Can Receive Your Blessings

I am convinced the Lord wants us to make a transfer: Our burdens for his joy and peace. In fact, I think the Bible makes that clear:

*"Give all your worries and cares to God, for he cares about you."* (1 Peter 5:7 NLT).

Here's another example:

*"To all who mourn in Israel, he will give a crown of beauty for ashes, a joyous blessing instead of mourning, festive praise instead of despair. In their righteousness, they will be like great oaks that the*

*Lord has planted for his own glory."* (Isaiah 61:3 NLT).

Many of us need God's peace. We have heavy burdens and soul-twisting issues facing us, or feel like we are suffocating in the hard times and difficulties of the moment. What I have learned, though, is that most of these trials and crossroads in life are *opportunities* to learn that we really can – must – trust God more with every detail of our sojourn on earth.

Some of us can fall into the lie that God allows these tough interludes in life because He is angry with us or just plain mean, even spiteful toward His wayward creations. The truth is, if we live outside of God's will and plan for our lives, we can bring a lot of this stuff on ourselves. Some of us are doing that, but *even then God is working for our good!*

A number of years ago I resigned my job as a youth pastor in another church. I took that step with what I thought were sensible motives, too – I felt it was time for me, Carrie and our family to step out and into a senior pastor's position in a church of our own. I was ready, I convinced myself, to spread my own wings as a minister.

Later, when I could look back on the decision with brutal but honest hindsight, I knew the truth: I had become frustrated with being a youth pastor and I felt like I was no longer doing a good job. So, I met with my senior pastor and told him I wanted to move onward to shepherding my own congregation.

It wasn't long, though, before I realized I had made a big mistake. The doors to churches looking for a new chief pastor just weren't opening, at least to me. Things were not coming together the way I had envisioned; discouragement set in – along with the bills.

I went from being certain I was ready to be a senior pastor to wrestling with a growing conviction that I had blown it, making an ill-advised, premature decision that had hurt my family.

Now, many years later, I look back on that decision and see it as a painful mistake. First, I left for the wrong reasons. Second, though I'm sure the Lord eventually would have moved me on, I believe I left that church – and what it had yet to teach me – too soon.

But you know what? God doesn't waste anything. He takes us where we are, dusts us off when we fall and, if we are willing, sets us back on the right path – His path.

That detour in my life proved to be a great, if personally painful teaching time. God taught Carrie and me to more deeply trust Him, rely on Him, seek Him, and to give Him our needs.

I am so glad God doesn't give up on us when we blow it. He will use our mistakes for our good, if we get up from the ground and follow Him!

God took us by the hand during that time, guiding us to a new position – one where we would learn of the great need for His truth and love to be shared in a place many Christian ministries had all but written off: Salt Lake City. The path He put us on those many years ago eventually led us to Life Church is particular, and we now count that journey and destination as the joy of our lives.

What I am saying is that God turns even our blunders into blessings – *when we learn to cast our burdens on Him and when we learn to give Him our needs.*

Joseph knew something about giving God his needs and seeing the Lord turn seemingly dead-end situations around:

–   He was sold into slavery when he was a teen-ager by his jealous brothers because God had made some rather remarkable promises to him – and they hated him for it.

–   He was sent to Egypt, where he began a new, apparently hopeless life as a slave.

–   Eventually, he was falsely accused of trying to rape his master's wife and things got even worse when he was thrown into prison as a result.

- Behind bars, he met two of the Pharaoh's servants there. He interpreted their dreams, which came true exactly as he said.
- Because of those interpretations, he eventually was called to Pharaoh's court to explain the meaning of dreams that had troubled the most powerful ruler on earth at the time.
- That intersection with Egyptian royalty lifted Joseph not only out of prison, but eventually promoted him to a position of trust, power and wealth second only to Pharaoh himself.

Years later, after Joseph's position allowed him to save his family from starvation – including the very same brothers who had betrayed him – another test came. When Joseph's father died, his brothers feared that now the time had come when the brother they had so ill used would take revenge.

But Joseph's trials and triumphs had combined to teach him an eternally precious lesson: God is able to take our worst situations and turn them into the best of outcomes. Joseph said as much to his brothers as he sought to put them at ease:

*"As far as I am concerned, God turned into good what you meant for evil."* Genesis 50:20 NLT).

We can picture the scene of Joseph's brothers realizing Joseph had forgiven them. Furrowed brows relaxed, knotted shoulders loosened up, smiles replaced grimaces. It was a remarkable moment, to be sure.

But it was even more, much more than that. Joseph's words and actions then established a principle of God's favor in motion. What he did — choosing to set aside the all-to-human desire to punish those who have done us wrong and to instead forgive and embrace those who have hurt us – was to confirm that God delights in taking on our shattered hopes and transforming them into miraculous successes.

He will do that, though, only if we truly give Him our needs and *quit obsessing about them.*

Joseph could have decided to be consumed by his trials, allowing them to capture and bind his heart in hopelessness and to fatally sour his spirit. He easily could have become embittered by all the wrongs that were done to him. After all, he was innocent! He was entitled to be bitter.

Instead, Joseph chose to live by a higher standard and to trust God. Joseph turned his needs over to the Lord and trusted Him with the outcome.

God reward that trust. Talk about blessings! Literally, Joseph went from the prison pit to the palace. What a spiritual odyssey he had taken, starting with the promise of God delivered in dreams, then into slavery through the betrayal of his own flesh and blood, and out of that despair being elevated to the pinnacle of political and economic power over *the* superpower of the ancient world.

You can't have much more of a roller coaster ride than that. But Joseph understood something it takes many of us all our lives to learn, if then: God is bigger than our needs. The truth is, if Joseph *had* gotten bitter or sour in his spirit he never would have realized the blessings of God as he did.

Too often, though, we are more like the tragic figure of King Saul than we are Joseph. When Saul was installed as the first king of Israel, everything seemed to be looking up for him. He was given promises directly from the Lord for blessings upon both him and his kingdom.

All God wanted from him in return was *faithfulness*. Sadly, as I shared earlier in this book, Saul failed that test. He was repeatedly unfaithful, and God lifted his spirit – and the promises that came with it – from Saul. The king's world sank into depression, envy and murderous rage. He was tormented, couldn't sleep and paranoid, mistrusting everyone around him, even his closet friends and family.

Saul unraveled, eventually self-destructing, literally falling on his own sword when the tide of battle went against him. The Lord had to find someone else to be His chosen king, someone whose heart would be fully devoted to Him.

He found such a person in a young boy by the name of David. The Lord looked at David and said, *here's a man after my own heart.* God made a covenant with David that there would never be an end of his kingdom and rule. And from David's line came Jesus Christ.

About that son of David, the son of God, the Bible promises:

*"Of the increase of his government and peace there will be no end. He will reign on David's throne and over his kingdom, establishing and upholding it with justice and righteousness forever."* (Isaiah 9:7 NIV).

There is a point in all this that we can miss with a casual reading of this story: All of what God promised David and has fulfilled through his lineage *could have happened through Saul.* It could be argued that is exactly what God had in mind when he initially chose Saul to be the first king over Israel – but Saul sabotaged the Lord's blessings on his life.

Joseph, however, *received* God's blessings by learning to give all of his needs to the Lord.

87

If we are going to receive God's blessings in *our* lives, then there are three *confessions* we need to make and believe:

- First, *"I believe God hears me!"* If you don't believe God hears you, you will never give your needs to Him.

*"And why? Because anyone who wants to approach God must believe both that he exists and that he cares enough to respond to those who seek him."* (Hebrews 11:6 MSG)

There is no shortage of people who believe God exists; sadly, there is also no shortage of believers who don't believe He wants to be involved in the details of their lives. To them, God is there but He is distant and uninvolved.

If it seems God is distant and uninvolved in your life it is because *you* have kept him distant and uninvolved.

God cares enough to respond to those who seek Him. The enemy of your soul wants you to believe that the Lord doesn't care; really, Satan will argue, God could not care less.

Remember, the Enemy is referred to in scripture as the "father of lies" for a reason. The truth is that God is as close to you as you desire Him to be! Like the old worship song declares, *"He's as Close as the Mention of His Name."* And how do we know that? It is the peace that name gives us in our hearts.

There are times when we all go through emotional struggles, just those difficult times inside. I'm no exception. I remember one time recently, as a matter of fact, when I was going through such a trial. But when I poured out my heart in prayer and invited Jesus into that struggle – *when I gave the Lord that need* – the most amazing peace filled my heart. I just *knew* then that everything was going to be alright.

The daughters God blessed Carrie and me with are now grown, but I can remember when they were little and would have some sort of hurt or issue or crisis in their lives. I cherish memories of them wanting just to hop into daddy's lap and have me hold them, telling them everything was going to work out. I would, and just my embrace and those reassuring words would give them such peace that they would often fall asleep in my arms.

Of course, the amazing thing about that is there usually wasn't much I could do to change the situation they faced at the time. Still, it made them feel good just to be told it would work out. I wasn't saying empty words, though; I had lived long enough to have experienced trials and their passing.

But to my little girls, what meant far more to them was simply being able to crawl up into my arms and feel secure. They trusted daddy to protect them.

That is the same kind of trust, multiplied infinitely, that we can – and should – have in our Father God. When we give our needs to God, it is like crawling into the lap of our Heavenly Father; He is telling us it is going to be all right. In His arms, we feel secure, even though nothing actually has changed on the outside, because His peace and security reign on the inside.

*"You will keep him in perfect peace, whose mind is stayed on You, because he trusts in You."* (Isaiah 26:3 NKJV).

God hears you. *Believe it.* So make that first confession with me: *Lord, I give you my needs because I BELIEVE you hear me!*

–   Second, let's confess this: *"I expect God to work in my life."*

Not only is it important to believe God hears us, we also need to *expect* Him to work in our lives and whatever our situation may be. Let me ask, *are you expecting God to work in and through you?* Do you believe the days ahead are full of victory? If not, you are in dire need of a new vision of the future because God has powerful things in store for those that love him.

Here is what Paul wrote in 1 Corinthians 2:9 (NLT):

*"That is what the Scriptures mean when they say, 'No eye has seen, no ear has heard, and no mind has imagined what God has prepared for those who love him."*

Wow. God is saying that we can't even begin to dream about the wonderful, awesome things He has for us now, and in eternity to come – *if we will love Him and live for Him.* Let's underscore here: Paul was not just talking about when we get to heaven someday – he was also telling us our potential is *this* life, too, for faithful and trusting believers.

Certainly, it is easy to see all the problems of this world – how could we not, with them ever-present on newscasts, talk shows and in newspapers – and wonder how any good can come of the mess we are in. But God is an expert at taking the negative, ugly and hurtful things of life and turning them into the most *incredible good;* if we turn those things over to Him.

We have His promise! Those worries and challenges that burden us so may not work out exactly the way we think they should, but they *will* work out for our good – and the good for the kingdom of God.

Some 2,500 years ago, three Jewish teenagers – Shadrach, Meshach and Abednego – found themselves at critical, life-and-death crossroads. The king they served, as captives of the conquered royal family of Israel – Nebuchadnezzar II, had put up a statue of himself. The command went out: whenever musical instruments sounded the call to worship, *everyone* was supposed to stop what they were doing and bow down to his figure.

The penalty for not doing so was grim and deadly: a quick trip to a huge community furnace and a fiery death. Burned alive.

But Shadrach, Mechach and Abednego were devout Jews. So, when the music sounded and everyone around them dropped before the king's image, they did not. To do so would have been a grave sin, a violation of the very first two commandments God gave to Moses on Mount Sinai: *"Do not worship and other gods besides me"* and *"Do not make idols of any kind . . . you must never worship or bow down to them."* (Exodus 20:3-5 NLT).

Their faithfulness to God, and disobedience to their king, did not go unnoticed – or unreported. When Nebuchadnezzar learned of it, he summoned the boys before him. He gave them a final chance to bow to his statue, and again, respectively but firmly, they refused.

*"O Nebuchadnezzar, we do not need to defend ourselves before you. If we are thrown into the blazing furnace, the God whom we serve is able to save us. He will rescue us from your power, Your Majesty.*

*"But even if he doesn't, Your Majesty can be sure that we will never serve your gods or worship the gold statue you have set up."* (Daniel 3:16-18 NLT).

The king was enraged. Suddenly, merely roasting these three stubborn Jewish boys was not enough. He ordered his servants to stoke the furnace until it was seven times hotter than usual; Nebuchadnezzar wanted to set an example for any others who might be thinking of challenging his rule.

It didn't matter to Shadrach, Mechach and Abednego. Those young men were committed to God and full of faith that He would see them through, one way or another. Certainly, they didn't *know* how it would all end – but they *trusted* God would be victorious.

God chose to intervene, and do so in a way that even Nebuchadnezzar couldn't doubt. When the king peered into the flames, expecting to see the three teenagers screaming in agony as they were reduced to ashes, he not only saw them strolling through the flames – but there was *another* figure in there with them!

The Bible doesn't say this, but can't you imagine the king perhaps rubbing his eyes. Then maybe he looked again, leaning forward on his throne, squinting to make sure. *One, two, three . . . four!* Then Nebuchadnezzar lept to his feet and blurted out:

"... 'Weren't there three men that we tied up and threw into the fire?'" His advisers assured him that was the case, just three. "Look! I see four men walking around in the fire, unbound and unharmed, and the fourth looks like a son of the gods." (Daniel 3:24-25 NIV).

Whether an angel or, as some Bible teachers believe, none other than the preincarnate Christ Himself, a heavenly deliverer was with Shadrach, Mechach and Abednego that day. And because of that miracle, a king and his kingdom were changed. Nebuchadnezzar not only offered praise to the God of these Jewish captives, he ordered that anyone who spoke against the God of Israel from that day forward would be put to death and their homes reduced to rubble.

That was the miracle. But it would not have taken place without the commitment of three Jewish boys who would not let go of their faith.

I don't know what you may be facing this day as you read this, but I promise you that *Jesus will be with you.* And more, when you expect God's blessings, His answers, His deliverance, those things will come as you let your faith soar upward and refuse to let it be dragged downward. *That* is how you become an overcomer in life.

So, expect God to work. Make that confession: *I give you my needs because I expect you to work in my life!*

   – Third, let's add this confession: *"I know God is working for my good!"*

Note I didn't say that Christians should expect everything in life to *be* good. Obviously, there is a lot of bad out there. What the Lord wants us to know, though, is that for His followers He promises that everything that comes our way will eventually *work out for good in our lives.*

Paul put it this way:

*"And we know that God causes everything to work together for the good of those who love God*

*and are called according to his purpose for them."* (Romans 8:28 NLT).

Ask yourself now, *what* do we know? That somehow, God causes *everything* – the bad as well as the good – to come together in such a way that it produces good for us, even as God is glorified.

If you don't believe that, then you *will* get discouraged and throw in the towel when the going gets tough. It was the same when God gave Israel the Promised Land; they had to decide if they were going to go forward trusting God, or not.

He had promised them a special homeland of blessing and victory – but they were going to have to fight for it. Would they believe that those coming battles would lead to victory or not? That was the real test.

That first generation of Jews who followed Moses into the Sinai failed that test, they did not believe what God had promised – that He would lead them to victory and promise. Because of that failure of faith, they all ended up dying in the wilderness; God's promise was fulfilled within the next generation, the faithless ones' children.

Unlike their parents, this new generation believed God. They conquered because they believed that God would be true to His word – that He would work out their challenges for their ultimate good.

Today, that is the same test we all face. Will you believe God will use the battle you find yourself in will result in a blessing? Will you trust God to turn that trial into a victory?

You've got to know that God will work for your good. So let's make that a confession, too: *I give you my needs because I know you will work everything for my good.*

## Chapter Five

# Forgive Me of Every Sin. Cleanse my Life Completely. Make Me Pure So That I Might Receive Your Glory!

" ***B****ut if we confess our sins to him, he is faithful and just to forgive us and to cleanse us from every wrong.*" (1 John 1:9 NLT)

Unconfessed sin. It can fester inside us, sickening our spirits and crippling our relationships with God. Indeed, there is nothing that hurts interaction with our Heavenly Father more than trying to hide sin. That approach is nothing more than self-deception, since the Creator of all, knows all.

When we try to hide our sins from God, it is not that He doesn't know every sad and sordid detail of our behaviors, thoughts and attitudes. All we accomplish is to build a barrier that blocks God forgiveness, and because of that, we distance ourselves from the blessings and favor He yearns to pour into our lives.

You can see why the Lord has made it so clear in the Bible, repeating the theme so often from Genesis through Revelation that we confess our sins and seek His forgiveness; this kind of confession is critical to being open with God, and for keeping the pipeline of His blessings open as well.

You might be surprised to learn that many Christians don't understand the need for regularly confessing their sins. They have come to the conclusion, somehow, that when they first said the "sinner's prayer" – when they originally asked Jesus into their lives – that from that point on they no longer needed to seek God's forgiveness for new transgressions that all of us, as imperfect human beings, are sure to commit.

Of course, we *do not* have to re-visit all those old failures of character and behavior that we gave to Christ when we originally sought forgiveness and accepted Him as our Lord. Those have long since been taken care of for the believer.

Through grace we are saved, the Bible says. And because of our inborn, human weaknesses we can only stand before God because of that grace, or unmerited favor. It is grace that God gives by allowing us the gift of confessing our sins, when we again and again fall short of perfection in our walks with Him. And it is by confessing those sins to Him that we strive to have a pure heart before the Lord at all times.

That's why I always encourage believers to *keep short accounts with God.* In other words, regularly admit wrongdoing to Him; don't let the sin deficit build up. Let the Holy Spirit speak to you through your conscience and in prayer, and when He convicts you of sin, *confess it right away.*

Don't let those bricks of sin build up, layer by layer, until they become a thick wall completely blocking you off from God's blessings and favor. Address those failures right away; clear the closet of all that junk, sweep the floor of your spiritual house – that's how to keep your fellowship with Jesus strong.

There are three aspects of this principle of confessing your sins to God that we all need to remember:

– First, *confession acknowledges what God knows, anyway.*

Psalm 90:8 (NLT) puts it this way: *"You spread out our sins before you—our secret sins—and you see them all."*

Really, we all should read Psalm 90 periodically, maybe even memorize it! This portion of scripture cuts right to the chase, starting out with a reminder of just how *great* our God is – and how small we all are in comparison to our Maker. Then it minces no words in describing how *holy* our Lord is, and how unholy we are.

Tradition holds that Psalm 90 is a prayer of Moses, and the man the Bible tells us God spoke to *as a friend* should have greater insight into the nature of the Lord than any other mortal in history. So, when we read in this scripture that as an unholy people, we all deserve God's judgment, we should be truly humbled.

But after setting the stage with the undeniable truth about who God is and who we are not, Psalm 90 concludes with a plea for grace – His favor of forgiveness. And it is within the context of these verses that we read how all our sins are spread out before God, even the ones we think are *secret*.

In such "12-step" groups as Alcoholics Anonymous and others, the fourth step is to *make a searching and fearless moral inventory of ourselves*. Along with that step goes a memorable quotation: *"You're only as sick as your secrets."*

Well, that saying has taken on the status of a modern-day proverb for good reason – it is true. When people attempt to keep their sins and lives secret from God, they do nothing but make themselves sick in the process – spiritually, and even physically sometimes.

As Psalm 38:3 (NLT) puts it: *"Because of your anger, my whole body is sick; my health is broken because of my sins."*

And in Psalm 32:3 (NLT), we are told again: *"When I refused to confess my sin, I was weak and miserable, and I groaned all day long."*

When we try to keep our lives secret from the Lord we do great damage to ourselves. We will become sick in spirit, mind and body because God has given each of us a conscience. Our conscience is one aspect of the stamp the Creator has put on our lives – and when guided by the Holy Spirit, it is what keeps us on track with what is right and wrong.

Our conscience is the "whistle blower" of our spirits; it convicts us – makes us feel guilty – when we violate what we know to be right. This is true whether you're living in relationship with God or not. You sense when you've done wrong or are going to do wrong.

Now we all know that sense does not always stop us from doing wrong; that depends on the level of commitment we have to serve the Lord. But the fact is, we are hard-wired with that awareness of right and wrong and it speaks to us in our souls. If we listen to our conscience, it can keep us from experiencing – and giving – a lot of hurt.

I believe that one reason people can become so extreme in their sin is they are so miserable in their conscience that they plunge even deeper into darkness in an attempt to deaden their conviction. They can become just plain mean in their misery, lashing out because of the pain in their souls. And even though they suffer from their sin, they refuse to release it to God; rather than confess, they choose to let their wrongdoing eat them up from the inside out!

This proves especially true for a follower of Christ who finds himself or herself locked in this moral whirlwind. We all fail, and that is one thing so human. But it is quite another thing to try to hide that failure from God or to keep on living in that sin. That is a spiritual dead end; it strains and limits our fellowship with God – and if we allow the uncon-fessed sin – and the stubborn attitude – to go on, our relationship with God can be broken entirely.

It has been that way from the beginning of the human race. In Genesis 3, the Bible recounts how our first parents, Adam and Eve, tried to hide their sin from God. He had warned them not to eat fruit from just one tree in the Garden of Eden – the Tree of the Knowledge of Good and Evil. But Satan success-fully tempted them by appealing to their pride: *You will become like God himself; eat the fruit and your eyes will be opened.*

It turned out to be too tempting, and Adam and Eve made the decision to disobey God. And, after they ate the fruit, they learned that Satan was telling the truth, to a point – their eyes *were* opened. But what they saw was a nightmare. They knew what good and evil were, alright, and they became aware of the burden of sin they had just put on themselves.

This "enlightenment" brought shame. Before, they hadn't given a thought to their state of nudity. Now, though, what had been a pure state seemed vile, even perverted. So they hurriedly donned some fig leaves to cover themselves – and then, convicted of their sin, they hid from God when He arrived for His usual visit with them in the cool of the evening.

Of course, God knew already what was up. But He went through the motions, having already decided He would give his creations the opportunity to confess – which in turn would allow Him to set in motion a plan that would save their souls, and offer forgiveness and eternal life to them and their billions of children in ages to come.

So, God called out for them. *"Where are you?"* Finally, Adam came out of the foliage to explain himself. *"I heard you walking in the garden, so I hid. I was afraid because I was naked,"* he said.

*"Who told you that you were naked?"* God replied. *"Have you eaten from the tree whose fruit I commanded you not to eat?"* (Genesis 3:11 NLT).

It was truth time for Adam. But even though he admitted that he had, indeed, eaten the fruit, his sin already was working inside his character. Adam sought to lessen his guilt by shifting blame to his wife, Eve. *Yes, Lord, I did take a bite – but Eve is the one who picked it and then gave it to me.*

Eve admitted the sin, blaming the serpent – Satan – for deceiving her. None of them escaped punishment.

The result of that sin was to subject humankind to the curse of death and eviction from its first, perfect home. Things have only gotten worse for human beings and the planet they live on since. Peace was replaced by endless warfare; perfect love with prejudice, self-centeredness, depravity, rape and murder; and evening walks with God in the cool of the evening with the company of demons, both real and imagined.

But while all that evil was unleashed by disobedience, the ultimate cure for sin – and rescue from eternal separation from God – also was set in motion. God quizzed Adam and Eve not because He was confused about what had happened, but because He knew that it was essential they owned up to what they had done.

Confessing their sin made in possible that they, and their offspring in millennia to come, could be healed and restored to relationship with God.

The Lord knew this was coming from the beginning, even before He created humanity and man and woman existed only in His thoughts. And God's only begotten Son, Jesus, knew what it would cost Him to redeem that failure. That is why the Bible refers to Him as *"the lamb slain from the creation of the world."* (Rev. 13:8 NIV).

St. Augustine and other Christian fathers have observed that God's perception of time is far different from our own. We, as finite (we are born, live and die) beings see time as a river, flowing from a source and emptying into an unknown sea. This is *linear* thinking.

But from the God's eye view, time exists as a universal whole: past, present and future, with all their possible twists, turns and detours appear to our Creator as one experience. It is a mind-blowing concept for us, but that's alright. If we could understand God's thoughts, He wouldn't really be much of a God, would He?

So, even as He created Adam and Eve, He knew they would fail, and that rescuing His beloved children would require Him to pay a horrible price by taking human form and suffering a bloody, excruciating death on the cross. Only an eternal sacrifice would do to assure eternity to His creations – and He would be that sacrifice, an act of love Satan could never defeat.

For Adam and Eve so long ago, and for us today, the key to a restored relationship with God is forgiveness – and that requires confession of sin. Sometimes, that confession should also be shared with trusted Christian friends who can then pray for you in your challenge or struggle. Confession of sin is the key to receiving God's healing, blessing, freedom and favor.

*"Confess your sins to each other and pray for each other so that you may be healed. . . ."* (James 5:16 NLT).

So when we cry out in our *Confession* prayer, *"forgive me of every sin. Cleanse my heart completely. Make me pure so that I might receive your glory,"* we are opening our lives – and our spiritual potential – to Jesus. That starts the process of God's blessings, including His healing touch on our bodies, in our relationships and in our attitudes.

This is the principle that goes with confessing sin: What we attempt to hide, we're left holding – we're stuck with a rotting, festering spiritual infection that sickens us in every way. But what we confess, we are healed of; God lifts that load of sin and guilt off our backs and frees us to serve him in the humility and gratitude that wells up within us when we are forgiven.

–    Second, *confession of sin opens my life to God's better way.*

King David knew the value of confessing his sin, as well as the consequences of trying to hide his transgressions. In Psalm 51:5-7 (NLT) he wrote:

*"For I was born a sinner – yes, from the moment my mother conceived me. But you desire honesty from the heart, so you can teach me to be wise in my inmost being.*

*"Purify me from my sins, and I will be clean; wash me, and I will be whiter than snow."*

God wants you and me to make wise decisions because those are the choices He can bless. If you are wise in the conduct of your life, God honors that – He opens up His vast storehouse of blessings and will pour them into your life and your family.

Confessing your sins opens your spirit to receive all of God's goodness *because the act of confessing sin admits that God's way is best.*

When Jesus Christ died on the cross He gave everyone of us the potential to be victorious in our lives.

That applies to *all* areas of living – *spiritually*, of course, but also *relationally* (He wants your relationships to be fulfilling and encouraging). It also applies *emotionally* (He doesn't want you living with anxiety, fear, depression or anger); it affects you *physically* (God wants to bless your health, too); and *financially* (God wants to increase your resources so you can have your needs met and be a blessing back to His Kingdom.)

All the great people of the Bible were over-comers — people like Abraham, Joseph, Moses, David, Esther, Peter and Paul. In many ways, these heroes of faith were just like you and me! Yes, I am serious. I know such biblical figures are put on pedestals as extraordinary people, different from us, and far above us.

Sometimes, I think the Devil keeps that idea going. He wants us to believe that there's just no way *we* could ever aspire to be the kind of people as those heroes were – to have *that* level of faith for *that* kind of victory. But it's just not true.

James, believed to have been Jesus' half-brother, wrote about one of the Bible's giants of faith, the prophet Elijah:

*"Elijah was a man just like us. He prayed earnestly that it would not rain, and it did not rain on the land for three and a half years. Again he prayed, and the heavens gave rain, and the earth produced its crops."* (James 5:17-18 NIV).

Look at Elijah's life! This *man just like us* did incredible things for God. In addition to the prayers James mentioned, Elijah had a showdown with 500 of the evil Queen Jezebel's pagan priests, called down fire from heaven and then saw all those baby-sacrificing worshippers of Ba'al executed.

Fire from God. Influencing the weather. Yes, Elijah was a powerful prophet, perhaps the greatest in miracle-working of the entire Old Testament. Yet, James says Elijah was just a human being like the rest of us. And if you read about his life, you will see that even Elijah struggled with depression, doubt, fear and lack of faith on occasion.

These heroes of faith became notable servants of God not through anything special about them personally, but because they approached the Lord *with honest hearts and lived in open confession before Him*.

These renowned men and women of faith arrived in such spiritually effective powerful relationships with God through their *choices*. They chose to be open before God about their shortcomings and failures. They weren't born any more holy or godly than any one of us. They were ordinary people who chose to give an extraordinary God their best.

These heroes of the Bible *chose* not to compromise; they refused to get sucked into the morals of the society that they were living in. They had determined in their heart that they were going to stand up strong and stand out in the crowd – to serve God with all of what they were, and in integrity.

It is no different today. You and I make choices every single day that determine whether or not we're going to live an overcoming life for God. No one can *make* you stay out of sin; no one can make you stay out of compromising, questionable situations.

There is no other human being assigned to watching you 24 hours a day, seven days a week, making sure you do only what is right. *Only you* can make the decision to go all out for God – to be open before the Lord, to be an overcomer. Yes, only you can make that choice to get rid of the things in your life that you know aren't pleasing to God.

Ah, but if you do make that decision the third blessing of confession becomes yours:

–   Third, *confession gives me fellowship with God.*

Psalm 66:18 (NLT) reads: *"If I had not confessed the sin in my heart, my Lord would not have listened. . . ."*

There is just *nothing* like living in vibrant, open fellowship with God. No one else can hold you as close; no one else can calm your troubled spirit like Him. No one else can ease the pain, bring peace like Jesus. My relationship with my Lord is the most important thing in my life! When others cannot be there for me, He *always is.*

Sin breaks that fellowship. Perhaps you have been there – perhaps you are there right now. There's emptiness in your life. You have tried everything the world has told you would fill the void, and now you just find yourself emptier than before – and longing for more in your life from God.

Recently, I read an interesting article about the elk and deer herds in the Pacific Northwest. Many of these animals die from malnutrition. That's hard to believe, if you've visited the region's thick, old-growth forests and high mountain meadows; vegetation abounds.

But it turns out that it is not the quantity of greenery that matters in the long run for these forest creatures, but the *quality* of that vegetation. Lots of rainfall means an explosion of growth – but there is so little strong sunlight to go with that growth, that the vegetation doesn't develop the key nutrients the deer and elk need.

So, wildlife scientists were finding the animals, apparently with full stomachs, but dead from what in effect was starvation.

The lures of the world will do that to you, too. You can take in all it has to offer but in the end it leaves you longing for more – dead on the inside, seemingly full of pleasure but dead in sin.

On one hot day during his journeys, Jesus went to a community well in the town of Sychar. There he met a Samaritan woman drawing water and he asked her for a drink. She was surprised: Jesus she recognized as a Jew, and she was from Samaria – two communities religiously and socially at odds.

*"Why are you asking me for a drink?"* she asked him. She meant, of course, *Hey, you Jews hate us Samaritans and we aren't fond of you, either, so what gives?*

That sparked a teaching moment as Jesus responded – not about the mutual prejudice those two communities had for each other, but the nature of true faith. Jesus spoke about two kinds of "water." One was the water the world offers, the kind that temporarily satisfies thirst – much like how the world's pleasures seem to temporarily fill our desires.

But the water Jesus offered – His blessings and favor in a right relationship with us – is the permanent, eternal answer to our lives' thirst.

*"Everyone who drinks this water will get thirsty again and again. Anyone who drinks the water I give will never thirst—not ever. The water I give will be an artesian spring within, gushing fountains of endless life."* (John 4:13-14 MSG).

When we confess the water starts flowing again – gushing fountains of endless life!

Here is how Psalm 66, which we quoted in part above, concludes:

*"But God did listen! He paid attention to my prayer. Praise God, who did not ignore my prayer and did not withdraw his unfailing love from me."*

That is what happens when we confess our sins – when we keep the channels of forgiveness, blessing and favor open with God.

## Chapter Six

# Lord, I Believe You've Got Something Special for Me Today.
# And I Claim It in Jesus' Name. Amen!

Among the Old Testament's authors, Habakkuk is classified by biblical scholars as one of the twelve so-called "minor prophets." But the words he penned in 700 B.C., a dialogue between God and Habakkuk, stands out for its central theme of living by faith – and the Lord's response to that commitment:

*"Look and be amazed! Watch and be astounded at what I will do! For I am doing something in your*

*own day, something you wouldn't believe even if someone told you about it."* Habakkuk 1:5 (NLT).

The need for such faith and response from God in our lives is just as critical today, some 2,700 years after Habakkuk wrote his short, yet powerful book. Today, God's people face a host of difficult, often crushing issues; they are battling depression, fear, failing marriages, health issues, the economy and on and on.

But it's hardly all grim news for Christians. The Body of Christ also has people who have found the answer to dealing with all of life's many challenges: Jesus. I've met many of those folks right here at Life Church, and it is exciting to read the praises they share with us week by week.

They tell us about provision amid apparent hopeless financial crises, of healings in mind, body and relationships, of experiences that God has turned from bad to their good.

So, that's the good news, church. Yes, we have brothers and sisters facing incredible issues – but we also have folks who have experienced God's favor and healing over their sicknesses, depression and fear; failing marriages that have now been restored; and poverty that is in retreat!

Here's just one of those praise reports:

*"God has given me a great job that I know I wouldn't have gotten were it not for the Lord. The money and benefits are what I need and it's within walking distance of my home. This is a major answer to prayer!"*

I will never forget the sister who came up to me after a Sunday service had concluded. It was not long after our church had begun making *The Confession* statement together on a weekly basis, and she was nearly bursting to tell me about the victory God had given her.

This sister said she had not only been making *The Confession* with us on Sundays, but was praying it every day of the week. When I heard her story, I could see why she was needing to do just that.

124

She had been attending Life Church for only about two months when she became a single mother with several children to care for. She needed a job desperately; God provided one for her shortly after starting to attend our church.

Still, she just wasn't making enough money to meet her needs. What to do? She could worry and complain – or she could step out in faith and take God at His word. She decided to take the latter course, and started confessing – and claiming. So on a Sunday, in clear terms and simple faith, she told the Lord she needed a raise of a specific amount – and she needed it by the next day, Monday!

Monday came, and she got up to get ready for work. She prayed *The Confession*. She was, in particular, counting on the concluding phrase: *"Lord, I believe you've got something special for me today and I claim it in Jesus name!"* In her case, she was believing for that raise. And that it would come that very day.

Off to work she went. The day passed by and . . . nothing.

Tuesday, she got up, got ready for work, and prayed the same words again. The day passed and, again, *nothing*. Wednesday, the same steps . . . and the same results. But she refused to give up; she held firm to her faith and continued claiming the goodness and favor of God in her life.

She was desperate – and she *would not let go.*

So, Thursday came. She got up, prayed *The Confession* and went to work. But this time, something *did* happen. Her boss was walking by her desk and he suddenly stopped, looked down at her.

*"You are doing a great job,"* he praised her, then added: *"I'm going to give you a raise!"* And he did – the exact amount she had been praying for. But there was one more miracle:

*"Oh, by the way I'm making the raise retroactive back to Monday,"* he said.

Wow! I never get tired of sharing that story, which never fails to stir my excitement for the power of confession and God's faithfulness. Sometimes, I'll be having a rough week and get a little discouraged. You know what it's like – you just get plain tired in your spirit.

Ah, but then I will start preparing a faith message for the church and it is amazing how my tired, discouraged spirit disappears. Trust in God and confidence in His promises flares from a spark into a warming fire when we start meditating on the goodness of our Father – instead of obsessing about our problems.

That is behind the solid advice the Apostle Paul gave to us in his letter to the Philippian church:

*"Finally, brothers, whatever is true, whatever is noble, whatever is right, whatever is pure, whatever is lovely, whatever is admirable – if anything is excellent or praiseworthy – think about such things."* (Philippians 4:8 NIV).

I also like how the Message Bible renders that verse:

*"You'll do best by filling your minds and meditating on things true, noble, reputable, authentic, compelling, gracious – the best, not the worst; the beautiful, not the ugly; things to praise, not things to curse."*

Too many of us can't take our eyes off the ugliness in our lives, the cursed things. That's why we struggle with our faith. But when we can learn to put those ugly, cursed things under the promises of God, it is amazing how our faith is freed to soar; that's when victories are just around the corner.

There needs to be a bit of warrior in each of us, if we are going to live in victory.

That sister who experienced God's favor in her quest for work and a needed raise was acting like a warrior, persistent and refusing to surrender. When her answer didn't come on Monday, Tuesday, or Wednesday, she still didn't give up.

Instead of complaining, she was resolute – once more claiming the goodness and favor of God in her life.

She was both desperate and courageous and would not let go of faith that God would meet her need. She was in a battle and determined to win *in Jesus' name*. And the Lord honored her, giving her the victory.

The Bible honors such faith and persistence, too. Perhaps the greatest example of that is the Old Testament story of Jacob.

After stealing his first-born brother Esau's blessing by deceiving their dying father, Isaac, Jacob was on the run. Esau was so enraged by what had happened that he had vowed to kill his sneaky little brother as soon as Isaac passed away. Jacob fled to live with relatives, married and had children, and was blessed by God as he built large herds of livestock and acquired property.

Despite his questionable character, God had seen promise in Jacob and chose him and his line to build what would one day become the nation of Israel. Still, there was the matter of Esau – and Jacob's fear that even after his years on the run, his big brother held a potentially deadly grudge.

But God chose that time of dread and uncertainty in Jacob's life to prepare him for a life-changing confrontation with Him, and a future of blessings.

So, after his long exile, Jacob, his wives, children, servants, herds and treasures were on the road for the ancestral home. But what sort of welcome could he expect? He knew his future depended on whether he could reconcile with Esau. As Jacob neared the home stomping grounds, he sent his loved ones across the river for safety and remained, alone, to face what was to come.

But it wasn't Esau who visited his camp that night. He had a visitation by the Angel of the Lord. It likely wasn't until later that Jacob realized this man, who entered his camp in the night and attacked him, was a visitation from God. Maybe Jacob thought this intruder was an assassin sent by Esau; whatever the case, they wrestled through the night, and toward morning Jacob's foe struck his hip, dealing him a crippling injury.

Still, Jacob would not give up. He literally hung on. As dawn broke, the stranger told Jacob to let him go. But Jacob, realizing he had not been struggling for so long against a mere man, refused – unless this being first blessed him. The angel did, telling Jacob that his name would from then on be "Israel," because he had *struggled against both God and men and* [had] *won."* (Genesis 32:28 NLT).

Jacob's faith and commitment had been tested, and he had passed. The Lord saw how serious his chosen one was about receiving the promises of God. The challenge had been, would Jacob give up when things got rough – or would he press through? That night answered the question.

Jacob simply would not give up; that warrior spirit filled his heart, and when dawn broke he had a new name and was no longer a victim but a victor. From then on, he was a changed man. The blessings of God began to flow in even greater measure through his life, and through him was born a nation God would use to bless the entire world – Israel!

There comes such times for all of us, when we have got to lock our spiritual eyes on what God says, not what the circumstances may scream. In those storms, we must claim God's promised provision – not, as Christians so often seem to do, give up too easily.

We are so easily discouraged when our prayers are not answered instantly. But many of what we see as God's delays are meant as tests to see if we will hold on to His promises and persevere!

Are we desperate enough to battle our challenges through those dark nights of faith, to hang on to God's promises by persistent confession of His goodness and provision for our needs? Are we ready to keep the channels of blessing open by confessing our sins, and not allowing them to build up as barriers?

If you give up before the answer comes, you have failed the test. You have shown you are not yet ready for the fullness of God's provision and blessing in your life.

It can take time for you to reach that point. Faith is a journey, and God takes us on that path only as fast as we are willing to go. For Jacob, it took many years – he worked at least 14 years, seven each for his wives, Leah and Rachel – to finally reach the point where God determined he was ready to take on the mantle of nation-builder.

Why should we be any different? As with Jacob, God will delay His provision to test our characters. And those tests are not just to satisfy the Lord, but to teach us about the level of our own passion for God. He uses these tests to mold us into the kind of vessels that are able to receive greater blessing.

God's blessings, untested, can be misused. Remember King Saul? His lack of passion for doing things the Lord's way led to disaster and downfall. So, He tests us, getting us ready to receive those promised blessings – and at a time in our lives when we will use them for God's purposes.

With the Lord, timing seems to be everything. Something Bill Hybels – the senior pastor of the Chicago-area mega church, Willow Creek Community – once said is right to my point.

Talking about the mystery of unanswered prayer, he had these observations:

– *If the request is wrong . . . God will say, "No."* I know there have been multiple times in my life when God said, "no" to something I thought should be a "yes!" Only after time had passed did I realize that my way would have been a disaster – and that God's "no" saved me.

– *If the timing is wrong, God will say, "slow."* Sometimes we have the right solution in mind but the timing is wrong. If we try to force the solution, the outcome is not what is needed. Later, as God moves the elements and people involved into alignment, the timing – and the results – are perfect.

– The last two observations of Pastor Hybel were *If you are wrong, God will say, "grow,"* and *When the timing is right, God will say, "Let's go!"*

The underlying lesson here? *You don't give up* when you hit the "no" sign or the "slow" sign or the "grow" sign. Instead, you let the Holy Spirit have His way and you accept His wisdom.

When the time is right – and *you* are right – God will be ready to release the answer – His blessings – and that's when you confidently make your claim.

I am convinced that God wants to use each of His children in a very significant way, one tailored to our individual gifts and desires. As a people of faith, He wants to use us to usher in a new wave of His fullness and blessing!

As the prophet Joel wrote: *"I will pour out my Spirit on all people. . . ."* (Joel 2:28 NIV).

God has chosen each of us to be bearers of His miracle power. He not only wants to show Himself great in your life, He wants to show Himself great *through your life*.

We have been raised up for this hour, this time. *We are not here by accident!* We are a people of *destiny* – and we need to stir up the faith within us and start claiming bigger and greater things. That is what Jesus challenged us to do:

*"In solemn truth I tell you, anyone believing in me shall do the same miracles I have done, and even greater ones, because I am going to be with the Father."* (John 14:12 Living Bible).

Let's be a people who claim those promises, in Jesus' name!

There are three requirements to receiving God's promises:

- First, *Believe in the promise*. Read what Peter told the crowds of Jerusalem who witnesses the Holy Spirit descend on the crucified and risen Jesus' praying disciples on the Day of Pentecost:

*"This promise is to you and to your children, and even to the Gentiles – all who have been called by the Lord our God."* (Acts 2:39 NLT).

In other words, Peter was saying, that outpouring of the Holy Spirit – manifested that day by the sound of a spiritual hurricane, flames of fire appearing over believers' heads and the sudden ability for them to preach the good news in languages they did not know to the throngs visiting from other nations – was available to anyone who hungered for it.

The same is true today. Whether we are talking about the Holy Spirit's power in our lives or some other blessing and promise from God – you've got to believe it if you are to receive it. *Just hoping is never enough!*

– Second, *Focus on the promise.*

When Peter and John were making their way to the temple to pray one day a crippled beggar beside the road called out to them for a donation – he wanted some money. But that beggar got far more than a few coins. Peter knew God had something better for him – *but first, the man had to get his focus off his shriveled legs and on to Jesus.*

Here is what the Bible tells us what happened next:

*". . . Peter said, 'Look at us!" The lame man looked at them eagerly, expecting a gift. But Peter said, "I don't have any money for you. But I'll give you what I have. In the name of Jesus Christ of Nazareth, get up and walk!'*

*"Then Peter took the lame man by the right hand and helped him up. And as he did, the man's feet and ankle bones were healed and strengthened. He jumped up, stood on his feet, and began to walk! Then, walking, leaping, and praising God, he went into the temple with them."* (Acts 3:4-8 NLT).

— Third, *Prepare for the promise.*

When Joshua was getting ready to attack Jericho, the Lord told him that he was going to take the people to a place they had never been before – literally and spiritually. But to be able to get there, Israel had to first *prepare itself to receive the blessing.*

Joshua addressed the people: *"Consecrate yourselves, for tomorrow the Lord will do amazing things among you."* (Joshua 3:5 NIV). In other words, folks, get ready for what's coming! And what came was the collapse of that fortress city's walls, allowing the army of Israel to pour in and quickly conquer their foes.

What is *your* Jericho? Do the walls seem too thick, too high? *Consecrate – commit yourself in faith –* and wait to see amazing things!

God intends to take you, too, *where you have not been before.* I guarantee this: that journey will be so exciting and incredible, that you will wonder why you ever doubted the Lord's desire to bless you, provide for you and make you effective in His kingdom!

# __Conclusion__

H ere is how you can prepare yourself to be all that God wants you to be, to see His blessings in all areas of your life – your family, workplace, finances, community, church and in the richness of your personal relationship with Christ.

First things first: Let Jesus know He is your king. Do that by *laying aside* every distraction as you seek Him; *open your spirit* to receive more of Him; *give Him your needs* so that you can receive His blessings.

And never forget to ask Him to *forgive* you of every sin, to *cleanse* your heart completely. This is how you prepare the way for Him to make you pure, so that you might receive His glory.

Then, you are ready for this powerful, confession: *Lord, I believe you've got something special for me today. And I claim it in Jesus' name. Amen!*

## END

226469LV00001B/30/P

9 781609 575434